Roots and Paths

poems by Maurice L. Hirsch, Jr.

authorHOUSE™

1663 LIBERTY DRIVE, SUITE 200
BLOOMINGTON, INDIANA 47403
(800) 839-8640
WWW.AUTHORHOUSE.COM

First published by AuthorHouse 09/17/04

ISBN: 1-4184-9364-3 (sc)

Printed in the United States of America
Bloomington, Indiana

This book is printed on acid-free paper.

Roots and Paths

for Harry Wiener
one of God's gentlest people

Contents

Prologue

Escape

My dear,
Sometimes you frighten me.
Maybe you are being too introspective.
All this thinking;
All this going back in time;
All these images,
Good and bad,
Taking over your mind.

All this thinking about the future.
What happened to enjoying today?
It keeps you from going mad.
Think of the old folks
And how so many wonderful things in their lives
Are fading and what is taking over.

These memories of your loved ones.
Try to retain the happy ones;
Put the others to the back of your mind.
Escapism?
Yes, for peace of mind and loving the present.
Am I misreading you?
Well, that's the impression I am getting.

[Sylvia Wiener, mother-in-law of the author, 2002, at age 88. Used with permission.]

Escape Hatch

I'm not sure what frightens you.
I only write about my life
And this cancer,
Which for me is neither morbid
Nor depressing.
It helps me get on,
Enjoy each instant.

I spend my days in peace
With horses and dogs,
Clean stalls,
Work outside, in,
For community, home.
There's lunch with my children,
Dinner with my wife,
Playtime with my grandchildren.
I sit silent in the woods
On the back of a horse,
Watch pastures green up,
New plants push
Through winter soil.

Writing shows me
Who I am, where I am,
Where I was, where I am going.
If anything, I am saner
Now than ever, enjoying
The whole timeline of my life.

Paths

Concentric

I circle around the edge, step within.
Close by the center, I move
Outward. Walking a labyrinth,
I move in arcs, progress
From the outside in, inside out,
Gaze downward, vision inward.

Circling the woods on a trail, I can see its heart
But cannot get there except with my eyes. It's only
By looking from afar, through the trees, deep
Into the forest, that I glimpse
What glitters in the shadows.

I stand linked with friends
Circumscribing a ring, open at the center. My eyes
Sweep around the outside, the core
Faces me. The space in the middle
Feels full from edge to edge.
Our banding together makes the pieces
Whole, center and edge fused.

Training Ground

I paid a price
to be among the chosen
few. The red and white
school bus
took me to the select school,
upperclassmen
took me to the back
  of the bus.
   Jew boy!
   Weakling!

Football
  without face masks
Basketball
  outside in winter
Boxing at age nine
Hymns
  each day in chapel
Latin, higher mathematics, physics—
the stage was set
for college admission
  a view of the corner office
access.

Separate Footprints

It was strange to see him
At a friend's house that night. Gray,
Looking like I remember his father,
He was the same as ever.

We had gone to high school together.
He was a natural athlete, star
Fastball pitcher.
I was team manager, my passions
Theater, photography.

After the blink of college, we
Country-clubbed-ate-bridged together.
Marriages and careers all started, turned
Directions we could not fathom then.

With spouses, houses, children, forty
Years have passed. His path
Was curveball, corporate, meteoric.
Mine academic, published, tenured.

So we stood, feet planted,
Looked at each other,
Talked small. Later, we parted
At the end of the sidewalk,
Our tracks so different
In the dust.

Search

Fever surrounds me in my bed,
perspiration
covers my body, cascades,
converges on the sheets below.
I feel there is something
I am supposed to do to break
free
from the disjointed dreams that
play with my
brain.

Within a fenced pasture, spreading manure,
my tractor makes a wide arc in the field, returns
to the gate. Defiant green sprouts
break the brown thatch of dried winter grass.
There must be something
beyond the ordinary
I should see,
heed.

Raw wind in my face, the dogs and I
look for the mares. When they see us, they don't
head back to the barn as usual.
Something is in the air, they run in circles
as if being chased. I cannot sense
what they sense, yet have the urge to
bolt.

Afternoon light slants in my bedroom window,
green metal bridges span the river to the north,
cars the size of bugs creep forward.
There are people out there
dreaming in the setting sun
looking for the way
home.

Synchronous City

I drive down Clayton Road, a string
Of cars streams toward me. Who
Are these people who whiz by
From unknown
Starting points
To unknown endings?
I cannot see through tinted glass, do not
Recognize the cars.
Why do we intersect now, here?

I walk through Chesterfield Mall.
People move past me and I
Peer into their faces. I cannot see
Through their sunglasses, do not recognize
Any of them. Where did we start
To end with each of us
At this time, this place?

At Barnes-Jewish Hospital, I step
Into the surgery waiting room,
Glance at the people around me.
Why is Ed here today?
Where is his wife?
His eyes speak terrible answers.
What forces
Brought us both
Here, now, to expose
Starting points,
Mourn known endings?

Prescient Path

Riding the ferry from Culebra to Puerto Rico,
I knew Mom had died.

I was confused,
    relieved by news
        she had rallied,
            was to go home.
                I made plans to see her,
                    but my vision
                    had only been off by days,
the visit
was to her funeral.

Days and nights before crumpling
skyscrapers, some had vivid
                images of wreckage, planes,
                death, flames—just bad dreams,
                until
someone pointed to the television screen.

Some visions cause us to knock on wood,
spit over our shoulder, say *God forbid.*
Right now, I have no clue, idea, sense,
but there are times when I feel
smothered
by images of what's to come.

Untried and True

They say odds are in our favor.
Explain
Then, so many dear friends, family,
Me all having cancer.

They say his cancer
Has a higher-than-average chance
Of spreading. They say
She doesn't have long to live.

They say
We should follow
A certain treatment plan,
That the survival rate
Is this or that, if you do what they say.

Riding through the woods, I come across
An old trail hidden by green summer brush.
I think I will pass by, but my body
Subtly signals the horse to turn.

Opened Passage

Having cancer spawns a new intimacy. Friends,
Relatives, strangers share unvarnished truths.
Nothing is sacred, hidden by guile, left to chance.

Catheter tales, woes, scars
From navel to pubis, scars to our psyches,
Pee in our pants, our beds, or where it belongs.

We get up the nerve
To talk about the nerve that gets it up,
Whether we can do it or not.

More honest with other men
Survivors than with our wives,
We tear away the cobwebs

Of myth and mystery
Until we are bare.
There is only one thing unsaid—
  The lingering dread.

Week's Path

Memorial for a two-year-old.
        Retirement lunch for a friend.
                Emails with other cancer survivors.
                News of a colleague beginning
                                                to die.

                        I take my horse to a nearby park,
                Cross meadows, ford streams.
        Squirrels dart across, scramble
        Branch to branch.
    Wide,
        smooth
                lanes
                wind
Through the woods.

Roots and Paths

Jonquils bloom in my manicured,
mulched yard. Nearby, the woods
still exhale winter,
bare and brown in the morning sun,
nothing green but moss,
leftover sprigs of grass,
the living and the dead
still one.

Leafless vines
surround us. Some hold
half-fallen trees in a tangled
aerial embrace,
others wait like snares
overhead.

Everywhere,
  scattered,
    splattered,
      peeled,
        broken
trees cause us to veer
from the familiar track.
An upturned trunk's
vestigial roots spread
like a large pelvic bone.
Another's are hind feet
ready to spring toward us.
A chain-sawed
hollow log is a cannon's
bore aimed our way.

When I look down the hill, I see
the path where I will be,
heading in the opposite
direction,
on a different plane.
I look up,
see a hint of where I have been.
Both are familiar and foreign.

A fallen tree, caught
in the fork of another,
becomes my rudder.

The Great Divide

Missouri Mowing

I wait to find two days in June
when the pasture grass is
ready to be cut
and the Missouri weather will not
poach me.
With the fescue in the fields
more than thigh
high, I wrestle
the Bush Hog onto the tractor's
power take-off to begin six hours of mowing,
shaving everything in my path.

Donning my baseball cap du jour
and sound-deadening earmuffs, I drive
along the fence line of the first field,
cutting,
circling to the right.
Three-foot swaths
mark my progress,
time moves as slowly
as my orange machine fighting
thick prairie.

Clockwise around the irregular edge,
the blade
spins in a counter direction.
Cutting from the outside in,
I travel an ever-changing
pattern, move from
boredom to
sensory overload.
From the house, the field
seems a block of green,
but hands on the wheel, eyes
opened, I see
vines
intertwined
with ripened seed heads of grass,

bright pink thistle flowers
risen in defiance,
Queen Anne's lace and clover
in gentle bloom.

Rabbits race from the uncut center
in wild
       zigzag
panic.
Bright blue-feathered swallows follow,
crisscross within my reach, gather
insects stirred
into the air by my mowing.
Dozens whirl and circle,
fill their bills,
disappear to their nests and young,
return
for more split-tailed dances.
A faded blue
pickup
leaves
the subdivision across the road,
hand mower in its bed.

You Have My Divided Attention

When do you daydream?
Do you miss
                    exits on the Interstate
        thinking of something else?
Do you wander
      in
         the
              middle
          of
              a
      conversation
          with the people you love?

When is your full focus on the moment?
Walking on a shady path?
Saying the blessings?
Chopping vegetables?
Does watching television
   or sitting at a computer
count?
What draws you away from
    now
to bounce on tangents of
               then
                  or
                        to be?

What brings you back?

In the middle of
      our talking,
      driving home from dinner,
      sitting by your side,
    these questions came to me.

Acupicture

Her fingers
press my forehead,
knead
tension from my temples.
I'm somewhere,
                          teleported
from her mind to vibrant
                color,
                  long-remembered images.
Through
her
as
        antenna
I
see
small, multi-faced crystals
                cascade
                    off a table
                            onto
                                the floor.

He twirls tiny needles
into my arms and hands.
Tree-lined,
sunlit
Southwestern canyons
spring into view.

I wish
this happened always,
with all who
touch to heal.
I want to
tune in
at will,
my fingers
on the dial
of a crystal radio.

Dream Journal

In a movie I saw, a man asked someone in his dream how he could know if he was asleep or awake. He was told to flip a light switch. If it was a dream, the lights in the room would not change.

> I don't dream all the time,
> But over the last few weeks,
> My nights have been full of images—
> Some earlier stories continued,
> Some familiar themes in new settings,
> Others brand new.

During the day, I think about whether I can determine, while I am dreaming, that I am in a dream.

> Nightmares wrench me awake.
> I am in cities, countrysides, buildings.
> I am lost.
> Labyrinthine roads, passages,
> Doors block my return.
>
> Or I am in a pleasant fantasy
> Sometimes talking with my dear friend
> Who died two years ago.

In these dreams it's always clear—we both know she is dead, even talk about it.

> Last night, she smiled, greeted me in a store,
> Asked where I would be for the holiday.
> She said she would not be there with me
> This year. "You know, there's not
> Much left of me anymore."
> She walked away.

I looked around in my dream for paper and pen to write down her sad words. I found nothing.

Snapshot

ONE HOUR PHOTO
The block letters catch
My eye as the small
White truck
Passes by,
Prints ready for pickup
An hour after drop-off.

For any hour I want to pick,
There is a glossy/matte mural
Of sights/sounds/smells/feelings
Imprinted as a snapshot
In my mind's eye.

Impressions on
Negatives,
Compressed digital files,
My one-hour photo
Stored for another day,
Or culled and forgotten.

The Glass Is Half

By chance, I saw him in the back
Row of the movie theater. In my mind,
His presence was a miracle—
Terrible cancer, little chance
Of recovery, then in a coma
Expected to die.
He awoke to slower speech,
Couldn't walk ten feet unaided,
But *remission.*

He hated his body—
Could never ski again,
Never stroll down a sunny fairway.
His anger dripped all around, joined
The sticky, food-stained floor.
I said I understood, but couldn't
So I offered to get him a drink.
He declined.

At a party, I saw an old friend,
Glass in hand. There was uneasiness
Around his eyes. I knew
From others his cancer
Was back with a vengeance.
A smile on his face, he told
Me his story, his
Odds and numbers and treatments
And no regrets.
He sipped his sparkling
Water. I sipped my champagne.

Thank-You Notes

At a local chain restaurant,
She sat alone at a table, busy
Writing on folded cards,
A pile of finished notes stacked nearby.
Waiting for my son to return,
I said, *Catching up on thank-you notes?*
When she looked up, I saw

Her sad and open face.
I just lost my baby.
Shocked, off balance,
I replied as best I could.
She smiled, *But they are
Thank-you notes.*
She reached out
Her hand, I grasped it.
She moved her gaze

Back to the pen in her
Fingers. My son brought
Sandwiches and coffee
To our table.
We talked about
His apartment lease,
A new computer program,
His photos of Forest Park.

Unexplained Absence

Three-and-a-half,
my grandson knows
        four great grandparents.
Seeing a picture of
one he has known,
        he tells you that she died.
What can he know
        or imagine
                about death?
                about life?

There are some he never knew,
whose eyes did not meet his,
        who never
                listened to him explain a game,
                called his name,
                held his face
in their hands.

What Did Gene Autry Really Mean?

What did he mean he was
     Back in the saddle again?
Where had he been?
Through my tiny TV window
He was always in the saddle
Riding, singing, catching bad guys
With his sidekick, Smiley—

     Time to saddle up, boys.
     Let's cross the saddle
     Between the two mountains.
     We're saddled with something hard,
     But we'll be in the saddle,
     In control.
     So, let's mount up and ride.

I am always in the saddle,
Legs touching flanks,
Hands on reins,
Body and mind directing,
Moving. I sit up, ever straight,
Eyes forward, feel and listen
To this animal, *life*.

I ride across the saddle,
Birth and death rise
Above on both sides.
I think I am passing between,
Then realize I have come down
From one, and must climb
The other. How do I want to go?

I want to be in the saddle,
Always in the saddle.

Rooted in Place

An Hour with Willard Abbott

We heard his horses before we could see them or him—
Matched Belgian geldings, gold-upholstered black carriage,
Willard Abbott in the driver's seat. He sat erect,
Four reins in his hands, nails clean and short. His polished
Worn boots, striped shirt, black jeans, and straw
Cowboy hat were as timeless as the sweet smell of leather
Harness, the restless stomp of horses' hooves when he stopped
The team. We climbed up. Willard told his tale with

Warmth and an easy smile, stopping
The carriage to unveil each story. Through all his life,
He has been part of this land.
He's lived here, hunted, run cattle, raised
Children and grandchildren. It's the place
He returned to after
The Bomb,
The farm he nestled into as it
Snuggled against the mountains.

Sure hands on the reins directed the horses
Back to the pickup point, kept flies off their backs.
Our minds were filled with the picture
Album he had spoken—his Belgians
Pulling a mower, cattle breaking into the old
Farmhouse, his table next to the trout stream.

Fast-Flowing Stream of Conscience

We jolt down rock roads into the field,
Bounce over familiar ruts to the bank of the Huzzah,
Empty the Suburban of children, dogs, blankets, towels,
      hamper of cold cuts, devilled eggs,
      apples, chocolate chip cookies
Arrange everything
In the shade
On the gravel beach.

Off with my T-shirt,
             into the water,
Icy on this steamy day. I take
A child's hand, move into the stream,
Wade almost chest high.

Current tugs at my feet,
Friends laugh, splash,
Canoes drift in the deep.
I smell the water, the air,
Feel the sun on my back.

Two black shapes leave the other bank,
Swim toward us in tandem. My shout
Stops all.
We stand
   perfectly
   still,
Watch as the water moccasins
Slide downstream.

Spinning in Control

The kinetic sculpture has crescent moons, stars,
Lightning bolts. Breezes whip them around,
Up and down. They squeal as they pivot
In the changing wind, saw blades
Poised to chew you up if you get too close.

Another sculpture
Has two smooth-edged, vertical wheels
That move gently,
Silently,
In opposite directions.

Deep Woods On

Take the familiar trail,
Empty everything from before,
Relax into the saddle,
Be present.

Look at that stand of trees,
Leaves turning color.
Lean back, look up to the sky.
The sun is still at a morning's angle.
        Salmon for dinner?

Onward up the hill,
Squirrels seem to fly across the path,
Obsessed with branches.
        Mail piled up at home
                We need bread

Toppled trees are dappled with fungi. A cool breeze
Brushes by, impending autumn smells damp.
                Doggone football team lost again
        Grandchildren coming tonight
                Terrible freeway accident

Listen to the wind in the treetops, like light rain.
                Will our garden survive the drought?
                        Sell telecomm stocks soon
        West Nile virus
                List of chores

Where is that bridge to cross the creek?
Have I gone over it already?
How did that happen?

A black and white butterfly rises like a dream from a nearby tree.

Stuck in a Paradigm

If you put your hand
against
the ground,
you can feel
vibrations
that grow
ever stronger.
But you can't
see
anything,
decide
the air that rushes
toward you
is a trick of the wind.
Nothing in view,
you walk onto the trestle,
eyes fixed on the ties, carefully
place each step
as you move
toward the middle.
Others
follow your lead, laugh, chat,
stop to squat down,
touch the thick patina of rust that
    covers the tracks,
    bolsters denial
    of
    what
    rumbles
    your way.

Delta

Diaper change
Changing weather
Lane changes
Change in scenery
              partner
                    health
Change in who's living

Our lives shift
        Transitions   warm
                        nurture
                        burn
                        maim

And what do we mean
        Why, you haven't changed a bit?

Clonts Barn Again

Three boys' faces peer out of the hayloft window.
Gray wood with faded yellow knots forms the old
Barn's skin, rough brush borders all around. The picture
In the album is changing color with time. My thirties

Son remembers that summer day with an eight-year-old's
Eyes. Four of us on horseback crossed the river,
Tread memorized, unmarked trails
Through the woods to get to this dilapidated relic.

Clonts Barn was a monument to some great
Grandparent's era. Even though we knew kin
Who could tell its story, we cherished its abandonment,
Well worth the long, tough, branch- and spider-webbed

Paths. Then roads were bulldozed, rocked,
Marked with arrows and signs. The barn was gutted,
Reemerged as a modern weekend retreat,
The hayloft a dance floor. Brush was cleared,

Woods gave way to landscaping. Footprints
On old trails were obliterated
By the tracks of yellow mechanical
Beasts. A simple car ride takes you there

For a cocktail and tour. But it's to the picture
In the album and in our minds that we go,
Our senses aglow, image still clear
After twenty-five years.

Side Walk

The land was half
Tree- and brush-filled ravines, half
Flat——a meadow with orchard grass, cornflowers,
The only building a rusted shed at its edge.
Rain moved over its surface,
Disappeared into its soil.

Now it's partitioned by pavement,
Pools, porches, patios, palaces.
Utility pipes and cables lie
Buried beneath sodded lawns,
Streams channeled, changed
To meet new desires.

Crews erect expensive
Brick or stone facades,
Vinyl siding around back,
More gables than the book.
False dormers stare down, revealing
Attic insulation. A stainless
Sewer-lift station
Sits where the old shed had been.

I walk around each cul-de-sac,
Along the concrete path
Outside its gates,
But when Tara's fence
Ends, so does the pavement,
Which leaves me
Peering
Gratefully

Into an untouched chasm.

Shrinking

Yellow stripes of straw dry on a field of green,
Winter wheat harvested in July heat,
Cut off at ground level,
Raked into mounded rows.
This crop island is all that remains
Of what once was rolling farmland.
Now it's surrounded by pricey subdivisions,
A Korean church, two-lane highway.
How long will this anachronism exist
As twenty-first-century *Westward, Ho!*
Replaces wheat with paved streets?
Suburbanites at the health food store
Consume their wheat grass drink
As fields shrink.

Gumbo Flats 1: Reasonable and Proper

The three-lane highway rounded a curve
Then rolled straight for five miles,
Heading west of where civilization ended.
In those days, there was no
Speed limit,
Just a sign that called for
Reasonable and Proper,
A way of setting boundaries
That is long gone.

Also gone, the Gumbo Flats, where
Broad fields flanked the highway
As it flowed
Toward a two-lane bridge over the Missouri.
You could fly
Down the unbroken lane
In front of you,
Whiz by barns, silos,
Parallel rows of beans,
A butcher shop.

Traveling across forty-five years,
The river valley boasts
A new name,
Restricted speed,
Unlimited development.
A six-lane, divided
Interstate leads
To same-width bridges.
Hotels, offices, fast food, a two-mile-long
Shopping center draw the driver.

The butcher shop is now a trendy restaurant
With gourmet deli, ornamental grasses.
Child-filled minivans
Feed onto striped asphalt fields
For indoor soccer, ice rinks, and tennis,
To explore homogenized
Retail boxes that line
Both sides of the highway.
A large airport, surrounded
By commercial buildings, expands
Where corn once grew.
Each concrete/brick
Structure erases the past
With the rubber
From rush-hour traffic.

Animal Attraction

Petaphors

Tiger

Our first feline,
Farm born, he adapted
To an indoor life,
Children
Who picked him up
At odd angles
Hugged him, hind feet dangling.
In a catnap
He leapt from fat kitten
To drawn, old age.

Piña

In the apartment
She was my only company,
Constant companion.
She watched through the curtains,
Waited for me to come home.
When my feet touched the stairs
I could hear her plaintive mew.
Later she would talk
Sit on my lap
Rest a paw on my nose.

Conditions forced me
To give her to a friend.
At my visits, she sat
Silent,
Showed me her back.

Orville

Sitting in the cold
Watching the stars
I turn around as if he were there.
Small, yellow, fuzzy

Barn denizen,
He died years ago
But on winter nights
I can still hear his juicy purr
As he emerged from the dark.

Dog Days

1960s: Voodoo Doggerel
Voodoo, our toy poodle, would not
Come when called. She hid
Under the sofa in the dark, bit
Any exploring hand. Had we put a hex
On this contrary canine with her
Bewitching name?

1970s: Dogged Free-Range Sabra
Our English Pointer pup was a born
Hunter, I wasn't. On horseback over old
Logging trails, through cattle-filled
Fields, she ranged out, nose
To the ground, circled back again. Long
Lived and loved, she died
Nestled in a mound of hay in the barn.

1980s: Cassie—Doggoned Witless
Dogless and of tender heart, we adopted
A Dalmatian who liked to run away
From her city home. I first thought her deaf—
She didn't respond without eye contact.
On trail rides, she disappeared
Over the horizon. Whispering in her ear,
You heard your words come
Out the other side.

1990s: Disney Dog Breath
Simba and Minnie, half-siblings
With revolting taste, graze
Stalls, pastures for choice bits of
Manure, consume them like rare
Truffles. Sated, they join me
On a bench in the barn,
Pant in my face.

In Passing

Bits of ice float by as
The mare picks her way
Across the shallow creek.
Astride, I watch for holes,
Snags. When she touches the far
Bank, I raise my eyes. A coyote
Stands just ahead, behind
The rusted four-rail farm gate.
His thick grey winter fur
Ruffles in the March wind.

Mown patterns of scattered straw
Shuffle underfoot as the buckskin
Crosses the field.
For some time,
The young coyote stays
Several paces to our right,
We going his way or he ours,
Before he turns,
Saunters into the underbrush.

Gray Morning

The dog diverted my attention
Or I would have passed unseeing,
Her fur well camouflaged in the bed
Of last year's leaves she had chosen.
She was stretched out
Behind the red Bush Hog in the shed,
Once-foxy eyes open but dull, teeth
Showing. She was dead but still
Limp, dry though it had rained hard
All night and morning. There were no
Marks of fight, flight. The night

Before, I read my granddaughter a book
With a fox hidden on each page—
Here behind hay, there by the tractor,
Always in sight somewhere, diverting
Attention from the main story.

I used a spade to pick
Up the small body,
Drop it into its plastic-bag casket,
Burial in the dumpster beside the barn.

Flown Home

They bring a tree
grown a thousand miles away
to plant in my yard.
At its top, a tiny nest
grips bare branches,
its deftly woven grasses
now brown.

Perhaps there were
speckled eggs,
baby birds to raise.
Had they flown away
before their home
disappeared?

Flying Turns

Intersection

Harried-hurried-late again,
Attention more on
Groceries, dry cleaner, day care,
I have no idea where I am.
Nothing signals me to turn,
Eyes, brain splinter,
I fight to regain control.

A deer brings me all the way
Back. A boy, shoulders stooped,
Stands on his front walk,
Looks down at the inverted
Corpse, legs stiff. No one
Else stands near or watches—
                    boy, deer, me.

Then I am past, the scene
Beyond my rearview mirror.
At my destination, I wrestle
The wheel, the desire to return,
Stand next to the boy.

With(out) Warning

She must have known something
was wrong, pulled off the road, alarmed,
died within minutes.

> She slipped, struck her head, never
> talked or made eye contact again,
> died three weeks later.

She had surgery,
nothing was removed—it had gone too
far. She was told they had taken
care of it, died surprised six months later.

> She had lung cancer, bought
> a new house she never
> slept in, spent a year
> saying good-bye.

Bumper Cars

They have both died—

We ran together
On toddlers' legs,
Tumbled in the leaves.

We rode the same boring
Red and white school bus,
Pledged at the same college.

Adults living
On the same street,
Our children
Babysat
For his.

He raised his children
Next door,
Would show up
Unannounced
To ride my horses.

Not close,
But always
Touching.
Familiar.
Expected.
For granted.
Gone.

Doppler Effect

His wife shared memories
Of how he'd relished
The last ski run of each day,
His dog tucked into his parka.
How he swam with family
Through reefs as stingrays danced,
Built his business
Painting bright futures.

Their daughter honored
What he had taught her—
  plain speaking
  personal values
  hunger for life
Spoke of
A first grandchild
Yet to be born.

A friend told of missing
Advice
Sought and received,
Times
On the green,
At his bedside.

While each spoke
  to us
  to him
I could hear
  his voice.

As those who love him
Extended his being
Into the room,
Gave tongue to his
        thoughts
        doubts
        passions,
I heard an echo
Stretching

Away.

Sunday/Before/After

Her circle of friends sits
Watching as she sleeps,
A shaft of blue-white light flickers
Down, touches her forehead,
Links her to a safe place
Where she can go to heal.

She was always the one who saw
Connections, asked questions,
Probed options others didn't perceive.
If she could open her eyes to us now,
Imagine what she would say.

Fine Whine

The message that came with the bottle
Says the wine will be at its prime
In about ten years. Aged a bit
Beyond perfection myself,
I'm taken aback.
Is this a sign
I'll be here
To enjoy the bottle in its time?
If I keep buying young wine
Will it extend my life,
Or will the bottles I put in the rack
Have another's fingerprints
When poured?

In a Family Way

Early Childhood Centered

When I was three, four, five,
I frolicked in the woods
Behind my nursery school,
Ran, hid, laughed.

Smaller than most,
In the woods, I learned
About friends willing to stand up
To bullies.

The woods are the same
Now, but different—
Less dense, more tame
Than I remember.

From the hallway of the same school
I watch my grandson at story time,
Listen to the children learn a new song.
I search for myself in old pictures,
Hear Mrs. Newman speak
Gently while I played make-believe
On my naptime mat.

Freud Laughs

Sitting on the edge of my bed, my mother
would softly tickle my little back, while Dad
called from below, reminded her they were late
for a party. I'd close
my eyes, fight sleep,
entreat her to stay just a bit longer
to knead
my hands and feet, rub
my fingers, toes.

I can close
my eyes
now, hear
her soothing
voice
as she
erased
cares
with her
fingertips.

I See London, I See France

I am wearing Mickey Mouse underwear,
the real McCoy—his red shorts
with big yellow circles in front.

You see me in my preppie
knit shirt, cotton khakis, loafers,
a style that belies what's under.

Trousers around my ankles,
doctors see the real me,
enjoy the humor, unlike

this morning when I got no
reaction from my wife,
a joke told too often. I am

Victoria's alter ego, my secret
hidden beneath a senior facade—
I am wearing Mickey Mouse underwear.

Gumbo Flats 2: The Pink Lincoln

In the eighties, his seventies, my forties,
I flew south to drive him north. His pale
Yellow Cadillac was waiting, full of luggage.
On the Interstate I set the cruise
Control. We settled in to chat
Away the miles.

Talk turned
To my teenagers and driving.
In detail, with as many gestures
As allowed at the wheel, I told of times
When, as their passenger, I "braked"
Involuntarily.
I wondered aloud if a parent
Ever gets over that.
        No, he replied.
Not even now?
        Not even now.

Okay.
Did you know that I used to drive
Your pink Lincoln at high speed
Down the three-lane highway
Through Gumbo Flats?
He had known
But never had said a word.

Locked in
Just above speed limit,
We rode for a while in silence,
Comfortable in our lemon leather seats.

Accessory to the Second

I have Dad's name, but with a next-generation

                                            appendage.

He has been dead for sixteen years—
The attachment is still there, confusing
Computer databases, where
My last name often becomes

                                            "Jr."

Being Jewish, I was not supposed to be named
After someone living, anyway. Years ago,
An orthodox rabbi asked my Hebrew name.
Not thinking, I replied,

                        Moses son of Moses,
                          Moshe ben Moshe.

Confused,
The rabbi concluded
My father had died
Before I was born.

They called Dad by his first name.
I'm still known by a diminutive,

                                            Buddy,

Implying I'm little, even though
Over sixty. Yet I don't want to be labeled
Exactly like him.
I'll keep
The marker that leaves me

                                    attached but separate.

I will honor him as he did me,
My identity tied to his in wondrous ways
Beyond genes.

How to Get to Carnegie Hall

It's hard when young
To understand the sheet
Music of life. Bundles of eager nerves
Allow us to compose and play
Symphonies of passion
With long rhapsodic movements,
Opus One and beyond.

My aging father told me
He would rather listen
Than perform.
He liked music to lull him to sleep,
Not arouse him by its stirring strains—
His libido had become pianissimo.

I didn't want to be told
That the music fades,
That the hormonal themes of youth,
With their
      presto tempos
      and encores
      would be replaced
By a role as supernumerary.
Was it like a pianist foiled by arthritis,
Or would the will leave with the skill?

Decades later, I am a senior.
My concerts are less frequent,
But I better understand
The internal fugue. The music
Moves at an adagio tempo.
Hormones that once played key
Instruments now sit idly
On the sidelines, sometimes ignoring
The conductor's baton.

I've found new music to score,
     Arrange,
          Riffs and flourishes
               to explore.
Improvisations replace
Well-known tunes with different
                    crescendos,
                        longer overtures.
And, as for all good
Musicians, it's practice, practice, practice.

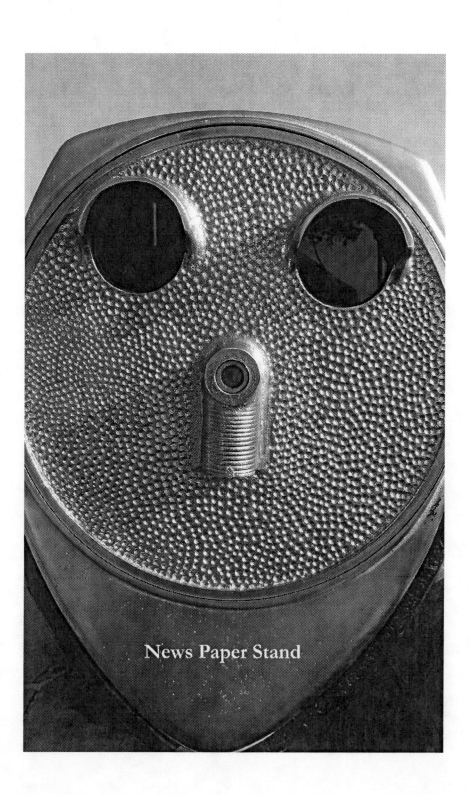

News Paper Stand

Foment

Three bucks for an inch
Of espresso, tons of foam.
Grande, nonfat, extra dry
Gives me a buzz to light up
Midday. Not much to drink, it weighs
As much as a feather.
They know me at the local shops,
Get my order brewing before
I reach the register, ask
If the resulting cardboard cup
Is light enough. I sit and sip,
Read *The Wall Street Journal*,
See which makes my heart
Beat faster.

No News Is Good News

Seven die in a pileup on a fog-shrouded highway.
A school collapses on most of the town's children.
Kismet, luck, or happenstance
Puts us in the wrong place at the wrong time.

Suicide bombers blow up scores riding a bus to work.
Anthrax-laden letters put deadly spores into the air.
A country's leaders impose their will on the world.
These are not destiny, lot, providence,
Not random acts or luck-of-the-draw.

We are heading in opposite directions at the same time,
Driving down the road, seat-belted in our air-bagged
Minivans, our young daughters and sons
Behind us in the latest child safety seats.
The television in front of them shows today's news,
As they toy with the loaded AK-47s on their laps.

Kurds in the Way

It's a heyday for retired colonels and generals
As each news broadcast strives to clarify what it can't,
Postulates on what will, won't, might, could.
I am transfixed by what I hear and see, become
A junkie even before our incursion

Begins. One of the third who don't see
Any rationale or excuse for what comes
Tomorrow, my voice is ignored, tread upon.
You can't buy my acceptance,
Acquiescence even, with a short, low-casualty
Expedition. Take a manufactured country, neighbors

On all sides with designs on its territory,
Ethnic groups. Stir it with fractured world
Bodies, defense networks, friends-cum-
Enemies. Add a dollop of destruction,
Beneviolent occupation. Some of the chefs
Lick the bowl. Don't slam the door
On the nuclear oven when you leave.

Siren Semicolon

The first-Monday-of-the-month
Eleven o'clock sirens
Wail.
I hear those close by and more in the distance,
The call pulsing
        louder
    then softer
            then louder
As the moaning machines pivot
On top of their poles.
This may not be a test

After all. There are sounds of apprehension
Everywhere
I look, read, hear.
I fear
I'm being told to duck, take shelter.
There seems no end to it all.

In the evening,
I saddle up and ride my fence line,
Look at each pole and rail.
The mare is unsettled,
Flares her nostrils.
I talk to her in a low voice.
Even though I feel as anxious about my world,
    I tell her,
      Easy, girl.
Two mourning doves rise,
Wings translucent in the setting sun.

The Emperor's New Fence

Our MBA president invokes
Cost-benefit jargon
To weigh
> freedom versus security,
> compromise my privacy.

A retired admiral, of Iran-Contra fame,
Wants to sail his ship through email streams
In search of hostile talk,
Anti-war demonstrations are discounted
As if they were marketing focus groups,
Those who don't conform are labeled
The enemy,
> un-American.
Joe McCarthy
Comes out of the closet.

Workmen bury a wire
Around the edge of my yard.
The dogs wear collars with probes.
I want to keep my dogs safe,
Out of traffic. They suffer consequences,
Learn to avoid
Moving too close to their boundary.

Saturday Evening:
International Velveeta

Vegetable biryani, garlic naan, chicken tikka masala,
Saag paneer—leftovers brought home to
Savor tomorrow. On the Sony, Michelle Kwan
Skates to another world championship,
Canadians dance, win,
Christie Yamaguchi advertises fast food,
Arena ice is filled with Russians training in America
And Americans with Russian names,
All caught on Fuji tape to scan through again.
Saturday Night Live
Is not,
CNN blather, conjecture, sights of Iraq
Are,
To be rehashed the next morning with George and
Tim interviews of Chirac, Schröder. Evening-ending
Doctored email clip shows Bush and Blair
Singing a love song
To each other—I play it
Six times before I remove my
Preppie polo shirt made in Turkey,
Shoes made in Mexico, some dissembly required,
And cover my head.

Kinky Freed Man and the Egyptian Jew Boys

Sitting on a hill tending the flock, he longed for a miracle,
Had a vision about espresso and Cuban cigars.
Suddenly, God appeared, told him what he must do—
Impossible for him
    Improper
        Implausible plan that
                Implied harm
                    Immovable
                    his people and Pharaoh's heart.

And he was right.
Try as he might, he was an old man
With a ludicrous message:
    Let my people go or you will pay dearly.
He would still be dreaming in the pasture
If God hadn't stepped in big time
With Moses
    Pharaoh
        The Jews
            Egyptians
                With Heaven and Earth.

More than illusion or magic
More than a simple miracle
More than anything ever before or since.

ශ්‍ර ඉශ ශ්‍ර ඉශ

Walking in my pasture, I long for a miracle.
Been to a café for my espresso, don't smoke
Cigars or anything else, don't really expect
God to show up here or anywhere,

Even as things avalanche downhill.
Impossible situations
  Implausible so-called solutions
    Improper behavior on all sides
      Implied threats to all of us
      Immovable
      my own people's and others' hearts.

And I don't know what to do.
Try as I might, I am an old man
With an older message:
  Let's get on with living instead of killing.
I am dreaming in the pasture. I know
Mortals will have to step in big time,
  But who?
    With what authority?
    With what end?

More people apart
More complex answers to visualize
More than a simple miracle required.

More than anything I have ever prayed for.

Seder Muddle

The Holocaust
Vietnam
Genocide
September 11th
Israel-Palestine
Corporate piranhas
Iraq

I seek a new Exodus,
Some way to slow the hurtling,
Engulfing destruction. No divine
Intervention—just a clue
Of what I am supposed to do,
Reassurance of the value of one
Person's role in the face of it all.
I see only traps, false trails,
No clear way out.

I sit in the light of the candles blessed,
Surrounded by those dear to me,
Pray tonight as I pray every day—
      Show me the way to peace.
      Show me the way to help
      Quell the chaos around me.

Scar Redemption

The surgeon made a six-inch cut
From my navel downward, removed an organ
Peppered with cancer. Before the surgery,

I took a picture of my abdomen—
This is what it looked like when I had
All my parts. Over weeks and months,
I found myself fingering the healing
Incision, a tingling reminder of the gash
Where hands entered.

I have wondered when the scar
And its sensation would go away.
It was red and stitched,
Visibly and invisibly. Later
It felt like braided cord. Then
Upper portions flattened, smoothed
Out, while lower parts remain
Raised and hard.

A year passed. I think it will not
Change much more. Now I realize
I don't want it to disappear.
I want to touch my scar,
Be reminded of what's gone,
Have feelings wash over me.

Acknowledgements

Over the past few years, I have had the support of several friends and family members who read early drafts of my work. They generously shared their thoughts and feelings, and gave me valuable feedback on content, structure, and word choice. I thank all of these wonderful people for their support and help.

Connie McIntyre is the person who really helps me hone each poem to its essence and keep grooming it until it's smooth and shiny. She goes way beyond just being an editor. She is a dear friend.

As with my first book of poems, *Stares to Other Places*, my son, Jeff Hirsch, provided encouragement and support. He designed the covers and the section divider pages, and also took my picture for the back cover.

And ever and always, there is my life mate, Marian, at the center of my heart.

Biographical Note

Maurice L. Hirsch, Jr. began writing poems in 2000 after a career in academia. His first collection of poems is *Stares to Other Places*.

He received an M.B.A. and Ph.D. in Accounting from Washington University and taught management accounting at Southern Illinois University Edwardsville until his retirement. He is the author or coauthor of several books and many journal articles, both in management accounting and in oral and written communication skills.

Hirsch is an avid horseman, breeding, training, riding, and showing Paso Fino horses for over thirty years. He has served for over twenty-five years as a board member of The Repertory Theatre of St. Louis. He is a founding board member of Chesterfield Arts, a community-based arts organization, and serves on the City of Chesterfield's Planning Commission.

Hirsch and his wife of forty-three years live in Chesterfield, Missouri and are lucky to have their children and grandchildren nearby.

Printed in the United States
93903LV00003B/346/A